Contents

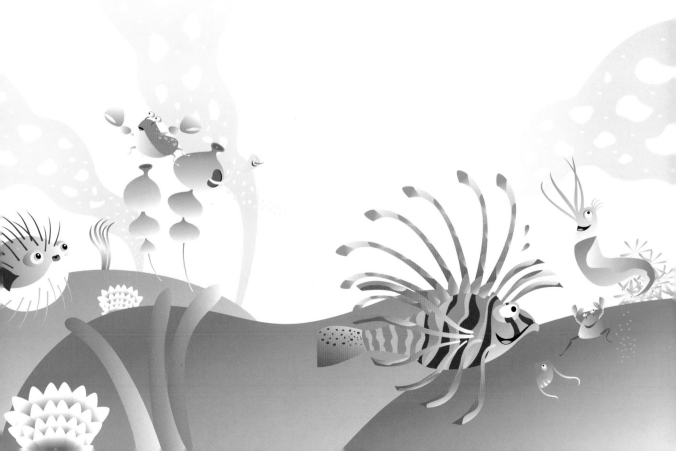

How to use this book

Each page has a title telling you what it is about.

Instructions look like this. Always read these carefully before starting.

Read these word problems very carefully. Decide how you will work out the answers.

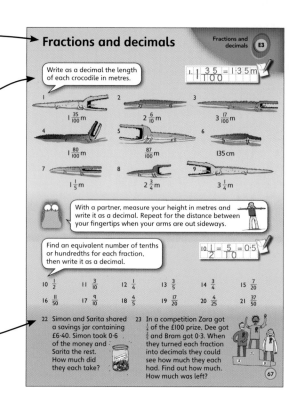

This shows you how to set out your work. The first question is done for you.

These are exploratory activities. You may want to discuss them with a partner.

This is Owl. Ask your teacher if you need to do his questions.

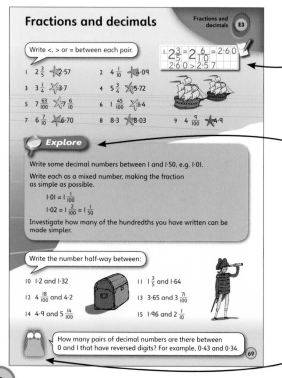

Negative numbers

Write the temperature 1° more and 1° less.

1. 0°, −2°

1	⁻1°	2	2°	3	⁻3°	4	1°
5	⁻4°	6	0°	7	⁻6°	8	⁻10°

°C
4
3
2
1
0
−1
−2
−3
−4
−5
−6
−7

9 Draw your own thermometer. Mark these temperatures.

a negative six degrees C

b negative two degrees C

c positive four degrees C

d positive six degrees C

e negative three degrees C

f negative seven degrees C

g 2° warmer than ⁻6°C

h 2° cooler than 3°C

i 2° warmer than ⁻3°C

j 1° warmer than ⁻9°C

k 4° warmer than ⁻2°C

l 7° warmer than ⁻2°C

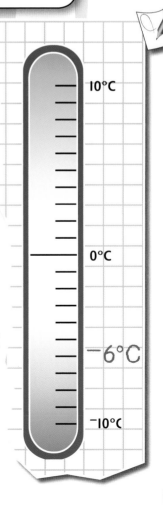

10°C

0°C

⁻6°C

⁻10°C

Write the lowest temperature in winter in your local area.

Negative numbers

Write the temperature at night.

1. $^-5°C$

1 Day: 5°C Night: falls 10°C	2 Day: 6°C Night: falls 7°C	3 Day: 2°C Night: falls 11°C
4 Day: 10°C Night: falls 14°C	5 Day: 8°C Night: falls 5°C	6 Day: 0°C Night: falls 4°C

7 All temperatures refer to Amsterdam, which is $^-1°C$. Write the temperatures of the other places.

7. Paris: $^-3°C$

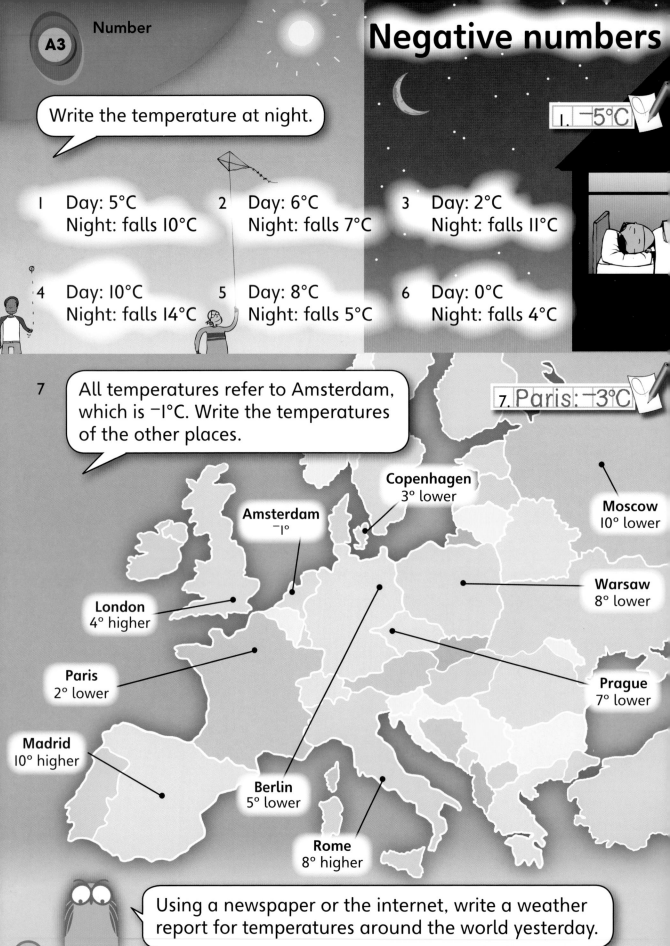

Copenhagen
3° lower

Moscow
10° lower

Amsterdam
$^-1°$

London
4° higher

Warsaw
8° lower

Paris
2° lower

Prague
7° lower

Madrid
10° higher

Berlin
5° lower

Rome
8° higher

Using a newspaper or the internet, write a weather report for temperatures around the world yesterday.

Negative numbers

Write how much each child has or owes after buying a ticket.

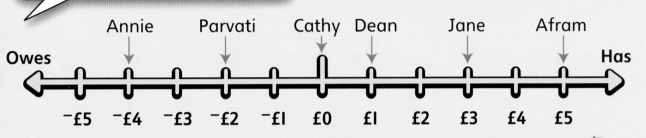

1. Annie ⁻£7

Owes | Has

⁻£5 ⁻£4 ⁻£3 ⁻£2 ⁻£1 £0 £1 £2 £3 £4 £5

Annie   Parvati   Cathy Dean   Jane   Afram

1   Annie  CONCERT £3   2   Parvati  ZOO £5   3   Cathy  CINEMA £3.50

4   Dean  SWIMMING £7   5   Jane  FUNFAIR £2   6   Afram  BOWLING £10

Write the floor where each lift ends its journey.

7. ⁻3

7   starts at 3, goes down 6 floors   8   starts at 1, goes down 3 floors

9   starts at 4, goes down 10 floors   10   starts at ⁻8, goes up 5 floors

11   starts at ⁻2, goes up 6 floors

12   starts at ground floor, goes down 1 floor

13   starts at 3, goes up 6, then down 4 floors

14   starts at 4, goes down 5, then up 3 floors

15   starts at 6, goes up 2, then down 9 floors

16   starts at 5, goes down 3, then up 4 floors

 Dry ice is ⁻35°C in a freezer cabinet. If it warms up by $\frac{1}{2}$° each day, how many days before it gets to 0°C? What if it rises $\frac{1}{4}$° each day? $\frac{3}{4}$° each day?

Negative numbers

Copy and complete the table.

Place	Start temperature		Up 2°		Down 5°		Up 1°		Down 2°
Warsaw	−6°C	→	−4°C	→	−9°C	→	−8°C	→	
Paris		→	3°C	→		→		→	
Birmingham	4°C	→		→		→		→	
Dublin		→		→	−6°C	→		→	
Berlin		→		→		→	3°C	→	
Brussels		→	2°C	→		→		→	
Madrid		→		→		→	6°C	→	

True or false?

2 The temperature in Moscow is −20°C. It rises 10°, then falls 10°. It is now −10°C.

3 When the freezer breaks down it is at −18°C. It rises 1° every 30 minutes. After 5 hours it is −10°C.

4 Tom gets £1 each day. He owes his dad £50. After 4 weeks he has −£22.

5 Jane owes Jenny £6 and Jack £8. She has £10 in her purse but really she only has negative £4.

Explore

Write the difference between:

a   5 and −8   b   10 and −4   c   6 and −3

Find some pairs of numbers that have a difference of 9 (one must be a negative number).

Rounding

Write the position of each pointer.
Round it to the nearest whole number.

1. (a) 4·2 → 4

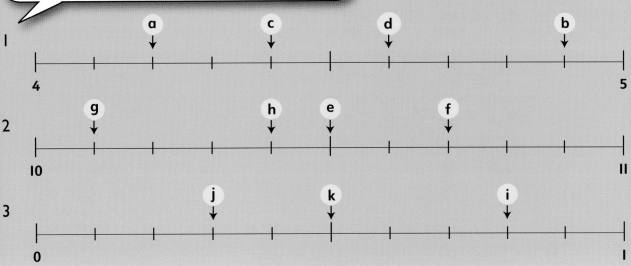

Round the weight of each
cat to the nearest kilogram.

4. 6·3 → 6 kg

4   6·3 kg

5   8·4 kg

6   4·9 kg

7   7·2 kg

8   2·3 kg

9   6·6 kg

10   5·5 kg

11   11·7 kg

12   8·8 kg

Two cats are weighed together. Their total weight when
rounded is 12 kg. Which of the cats above could it be?

Rounding

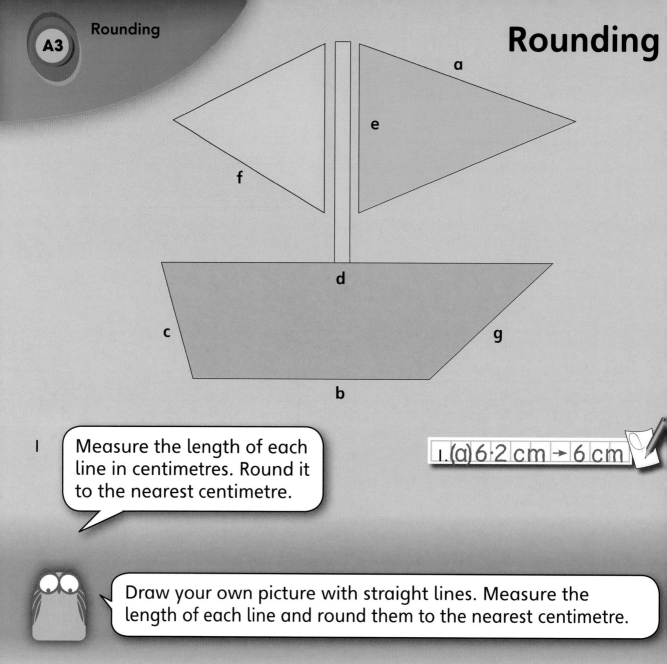

1 Measure the length of each line in centimetres. Round it to the nearest centimetre.

1. (a) 6·2 cm → 6 cm

Draw your own picture with straight lines. Measure the length of each line and round them to the nearest centimetre.

2 Write the position of each pointer. Round it to the nearest whole number.

2. (a) 2·6 2 → 3

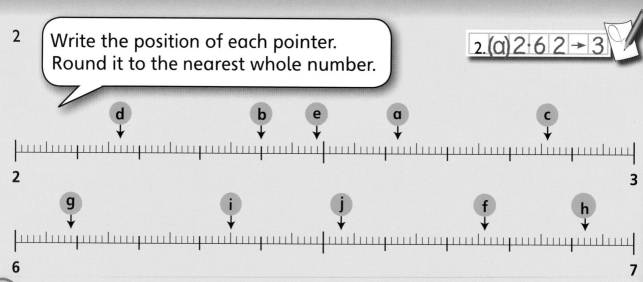

Rounding

Write each amount and round it to the nearest pound.

1. £4·76 → £5

1

2

3

4

5

6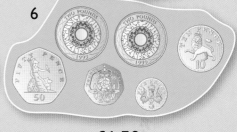

7 £7·09   8 £5·97   9 £60·10   10 £4·50

11 £0·82   12 £1·04   13 £2·22   14 £0·34

Explore

You have one of each of these:

Here is an amount that rounds to £4:

Here is an amount that rounds to £11:

Investigate ways of making amounts that round to each of £1, £2, ..., £20.
Using just four coins, can you still make amounts that round to each of £1, £2, ..., £20?

Rounding

Tim

Kim

12·37 s
15·64 s

Kat

Pat

15·14 s
12·88 s

Ben

Den

13·36 s
14·49 s

Sam

Pam

11·59 s
16·32 s

Each person runs 100 m. Write the time, rounded to the nearest second, for:

1. 12·37 → 12 s

1 Tim	2 Sam	3 Pat	4 Ben	5 Kim	6 Den

In the relay, the time for each pair of runners is added.
Write the total times, rounded to the nearest second, for:

7 Tim and Kim	8 Sam and Pam	9 Ben and Den

In the relay, who came: 10 first   11 third   12 last?

 Explore

Ruth and Ian each have an amount of money.

To the nearest pound, Ruth has £4 and Ian has £6.

The total of Ruth and Ian's amounts does not round to £10.

What could the amounts be? Give some examples.

Can you explain why?

Multiplying

1	2	3	4	5	6	7	8	9	10
2	4	6	8	10	12	14	16	18	20
3	6	9	12	15	18	21	24	27	30
4	8	12	16	20	24	28	32	36	40
5	10	15	20	25	30	35	40	45	50

Copy and complete. Sometimes the grid will help you.

1. $3 \times 7 = 21$

1   $3 \times 7 =$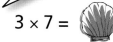

2   $6 \times 7 =$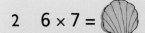

3   $9 \times 7 =$

4   $3 \times 9 =$

5   $6 \times 5 =$

6   $6 \times 8 =$

7   $7 \times 8 =$

8   $5 \times 9 =$

9   $6 \times 9 =$

10   $5 \times 8 =$

11   $3 \times 6 =$

12   $3 \times 8 =$

13

Use this grid. Use doubling to complete the grid for the multiples of 12, 14 and 16.

6	12	18	24	30	36	42	48	54	60
7	14	21	28	35	42	49	56	63	70
8	16	24	32	40	48	56	64	72	80

12									
14									
16									

Copy and complete. Use the grid to help you.

14   $7 \times 14 = \boxed{}$

15   $4 \times 16 = \boxed{}$

16   $9 \times 12 = \boxed{}$

17   $8 \times 16 = \boxed{}$

18   $9 \times 14 = \boxed{}$

19   $7 \times 16 = \boxed{}$

20   $5 \times 12 = \boxed{}$

21   $6 \times 14 = \boxed{}$

22   $6 \times 16 = \boxed{}$

Use doubling to write tables bigger than the 25 times table, for example the 28 times table.

Multiplying

Use the multiplication square to help you complete these multiplication tables.

1	2	3	4	5	6	7	8	9	10
2	4	6	8	10	12	14	16	18	20
3	6	9	12	15	18	21	24	27	30
4	8	12	16	20	24	28	32	36	40
5	10	15	20	25	30	35	40	45	50
6	12	18	24	30	36	42	48	54	60
7	14	21	28	35	42	49	56	63	70
8	16	24	32	40	48	56	64	72	80
9	18	27	36	45	54	63	72	81	90
10	20	30	40	50	60	70	80	90	100

1 $1 \times 18 = 18$

$2 \times 18 = \boxed{}$

$3 \times 18 = \boxed{}$

$4 \times 18 = \boxed{}$

$5 \times 18 = \boxed{}$

$6 \times 18 = \boxed{}$

$7 \times 18 = \boxed{}$

$8 \times 18 = \boxed{}$

2 $1 \times 13 = 13$

$2 \times 13 = \boxed{}$

$3 \times 13 = \boxed{}$

$4 \times 13 = \boxed{}$

$5 \times 13 = \boxed{}$

$6 \times 13 = \boxed{}$

$7 \times 13 = \boxed{}$

$8 \times 13 = \boxed{}$

3 $1 \times 17 = 17$

$2 \times 17 = \boxed{}$

$3 \times 17 = \boxed{}$

$4 \times 17 = \boxed{}$

$5 \times 17 = \boxed{}$

$6 \times 17 = \boxed{}$

Say a big multiplication, e.g. 9×14. How quickly can your partner give an answer? How did they do it?

Copy and complete the table to show the numbers coming out of each machine.

4.
In		1	3	2	4	
Out	2	7	3			

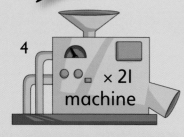

4 × 21 machine

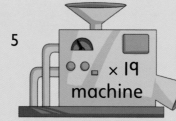

5 × 19 machine

In	13	24	43	16	27	52	51	19
Out								

6 28 children each give 13p to a charity. How much is collected?

7 Which is the larger: 17×19 or 21×16? By how much?

Multiplying

Copy and complete.

1. $(26 \times 20) + (26 \times 1) =$
   $520 + 26 = 546$

1. $26 \times 21 = (26 \times \boxed{}) + (26 \times 1) = \boxed{}$

2. $37 \times 19 = (37 \times \boxed{}) - (37 \times \boxed{}) = \boxed{}$

3. $52 \times 18 = (52 \times \boxed{}) - (52 \times \boxed{}) = \boxed{}$

4. $63 \times 42 = (63 \times \boxed{}) + (63 \times \boxed{}) = \boxed{}$

5. $34 \times 38 = \boxed{}$ 6. $46 \times 46 = \boxed{}$ 7. $28 \times 17 = \boxed{}$

Find the cost of sending these:

8. $21 \times 13 = (20 \times 13) + (1 \times 13)$
   $= 260 + 13$
   $= 273 = £2·73$

	Second class	First class	Express
21 letters	8 13p	9 28p	10 32p
31 packets 	11 14p	12 55p	13 72p
19 parcels	14 27p	15 61p	16 86p

 You have £10 to spend on postage. How many letters can you send first class? Second class?

Multiplying

6	12	18	24	30	36	42	48	54	60
7	14	21	28	35	42	49	56	63	70

Use the grid. Use doubling to find:

$1. 4 \times 6 = 24, ...$

1 $4 \times 6 = \boxed{}$, $4 \times 12 = \boxed{}$, $4 \times 24 = \boxed{}$, $4 \times 48 = \boxed{}$, $4 \times 96 = \boxed{}$

2 $7 \times 14 = \boxed{}$, $7 \times 28 = \boxed{}$, $7 \times 56 = \boxed{}$, $7 \times 112 = \boxed{}$

3 $6 \times 48 = \boxed{}$ 4 $6 \times 56 = \boxed{}$ 5 $8 \times 96 = \boxed{}$ 6 $9 \times 112 = \boxed{}$

7 How many 7s in: a 84   b 112   c 140?

8 How many 6s in: a 96   b 108   c 126?

True or false?

9 To multiply a number by 9, I can multiply by 4, and by 5, then add the results.

10 To multiply a number by 14, I can multiply it by 7, then double the answer.

11 To multiply a number by 29, I can multiply it by 30, then add the number.

12 To multiply by 30, I can multiply by 3 and then by 10.

13 To multiply by 20, I can either double it and multiply by 10, or I can multiply it by 10, then double it.

Explore

To multiply a number by 15: 38×15
- multiply it by 10   380
- halve it   190
- add the two parts together   570

Use this to calculate 15×18, 15×26 and 15×32.

Multiplying

Copy and complete.

1.
```
      4  0·6
  3 | 2 | 8        | 2 0·0
                 +   | 1·8
                     | 3·8
  3 × 4·6 = | 3·8
```

1.
```
     4    0·6
 3 [   ][   ]
```

2.
```
     2    0·7
 4 [   ][   ]
```

3.
```
     3    0·4
 7 [   ][   ]
```

4.
```
     5    0·9
 8 [   ][   ]
```

5.
```
     6    0·8
 6 [   ][   ]
```

6.
```
     7    0·4
 q [   ][   ]
```

7.
```
     6    0·3
 5 [   ][   ]
```

8.
```
     7    0·2
 7 [   ][   ]
```

9.
```
     5    0·6
 6 [   ][   ]
```

Multiply each number by 7.

10.
```
       6   0·3
   7 | 4 | 2 | 1        4 2·0
                     +    2·1
                         4 4·1
   7 × 6·3 = 4 4·1
```

10. [6] · [3]

11. [4] · [6]

12. [7] · [4]

13. · [7] [q]

14. · [8] [5]

15. · [3] [8]

16. [5] · [4]

17. [8] · [4]

18. · [6] [5]

19. [3] · [2]

Try this multiplication: 7 × [   ] · [   ] = 20.
How close can you get?

Multiplying

Find the multiplication shown by each rectangle.

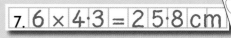

1.
	6	0·3	
4	24	1·2	

4 × 6·3 = 25·2

1
4	24	1.2

2
6	42	2.4

3
7	21	6.3

4
8	40	6.4

5
3	24	2.1

6
6	42	1.8

Write the height of each stack of tins.

7. 6 × 4·3 = 25·8 cm

7
4·3 cm
6 tins

8
6·8 cm
4 tins

9
3·8 cm
7 tins

10
4·7 cm
8 tins

11
5·2 cm
6 tins

12
3·4 cm
9 tins

My stack of tins is 32·9 cm high. Which of the tins above could it be made from? Invent a question like this for your friend to answer.

Multiplying

Complete these multiplications.

				1. 7×4.6	$7 \times 4.0 = 28.0$
					$7 \times 0.6 = 4.2$
					$7 \times 4.6 = 32.2$

1 7×4.6

2 4×7.4

3 3×8.6

4 8×4.9

5 6×5.7

6 9×3.8

7 7×6.4

8 8×9.4

9 6×7.9

10 9×5.2

11 7×3.6

12 8×5.7

Write the weight of each.

13 6 packs

14 4 packs

15 7 packs

4·2 kg

2·7 kg

3·8 kg

16 8 packs of cola
1·6 kg each

17 7 packs of tonic
2·4 kg each

18 5 packs of smoothies
6·8 kg each

19 8 packs of juice
4·9 kg each

20 3 packs of squash
5·7 kg each

21 9 packs of milk
3·3 kg each

Explore

Multiply ☐ . ☐ × ☐

What is the largest answer you can make, using the digits 6, 7 and 8?

What is the smallest answer you can make?

Multiplying

Complete these multiplications, then use a calculator to check by dividing.

1.	$9 \times 4 \cdot 7$	9×4	$= \ldots$
		$9 \times 0 \cdot 7$	$= \ldots$
		$9 \times 4 \cdot 7$	$= \ldots$
		$42 \cdot 3 \div 9$	$= \ldots$

1   $9 \times 4 \cdot 7 = \boxed{}$

2   $8 \times 3 \cdot 4 = \boxed{}$

3   $6 \times 5 \cdot 2 = \boxed{}$

4   $7 \times 8 \cdot 6 = \boxed{}$

5   $4 \times 9 \cdot 3 = \boxed{}$

6   $5 \times 4 \cdot 3 = \boxed{}$

7   $8 \times 3 \cdot 9 = \boxed{}$

8   $6 \times 7 \cdot 6 = \boxed{}$

9   $7 \times 6 \cdot 4 = \boxed{}$

Correct any errors.

Explore

Investigate the perimeter of regular polygons that have a side of length 4·7 cm.

Estimate the largest and smallest of each set. Complete the multiplications and put them in order. Were you correct?

10	$3 \cdot 6 \times 4$	$5 \cdot 2 \times 5$	$4 \cdot 3 \times 7$	$2 \cdot 8 \times 9$
11	$4 \cdot 2 \times 6$	$7 \cdot 9 \times 3$	$5 \cdot 8 \times 4$	$2 \cdot 7 \times 8$
12	$6 \cdot 3 \times 5$	$4 \cdot 4 \times 7$	$9 \cdot 2 \times 3$	$2 \cdot 8 \times 9$
13	$4 \cdot 9 \times 4$	$9 \cdot 3 \times 2$	$4 \cdot 2 \times 5$	$2 \cdot 7 \times 8$
14	$8 \cdot 7 \times 6$	$5 \cdot 4 \times 9$	$6 \cdot 6 \times 8$	$7 \cdot 3 \times 7$

Adding

Jamie  836

Kulpreet  342

Ling  778

Emma  564

Mark 657

Find the total scores for:

1.
```
  1 1 0 0
    8 3 6
+   3 4 2
  1 1 7 8
```

1   Jamie and Kulpreet   2   Ling and Emma

3   Emma and Mark   4   Ling and Kulpreet

5   Out of all the children, which pair has the largest score? What is it?

6   Out of all the children, which pair has the lowest score? What is it?

Copy and complete.

7.
```
  9 0 0 0
  4 6 5 0
+ 3 7 2 5
  8 3 7 5
      1
```

7
```
  4 6 5 0
+ 3 7 2 5
─────────
```

8
```
  5 6 7 1
+ 3 1 5 7
─────────
```

9
```
  3 7 1 2
+ 2 8 3 4
─────────
```

10
```
  6 1 7 2
+ 2 5 1 9
```

11
```
  4 3 8 4
+ 3 5 7 5
```

12
```
  3 9 4 2
+ 1 4 3 6
```

13
```
  6 7 4 2
+ 2 6 3 7
```

14
```
  4 2 3 5
+ 3 4 1 7
```

15
```
  5 1 8 0
+ 4 7 5 6
```

 What digits can make this calculation work?

```
    ☐ 3 ☐ 3
+   3 ☐ 3 ☐
───────────
  1 0 0 0 0
```

Adding

The space ship jumps into hyperspace! How many light years does it travel each time?

```
1.   9 0 0 0
     4 7 6 2
   + 3 9 5 8
     8 7 2 0  light
     1 1 1    years
```

1   4762 light years, then 3958 light years

2   6498 light years, then 5756 light years

3   6481 light years, then 3588 light years

4   6872 light years, then 4954 light years

5   3762 light years, then 4958 light years

6   6234 light years, then 5978 light years

Write how many years between the two dates.

```
7.   3 0 0 0
     1 9 2 7
   + 1 3 2 7
     3 2 5 4  years
     1   1
```

7
Tutankhamun
Buried 1327 BCE
Discovered 1927

8
Yin Ruins
Built 1236 BCE
Discovered 1898

9
Palace at Knossos
Built 2136 BCE
Discovered 1900

10
Ramses II
Buried 1212 BCE
Discovered 1881

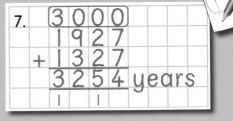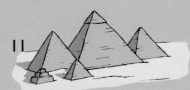

11
Pyramids
Built 2561 BCE
Excavated 1954

Think of films set in BCE times. Estimate the date they were set and the dates they were made. What is the difference?

Adding

Car A
£3468

Car B
£4759

Car C
£3976

Car D
£5267

```
  £ 3 4 6 8
  £ 5 2 6 7
+ £ 2 9 7 5
  £ 1 1 7 1 0
      1 2 2
```

Car E
£2975

Car F
£5817

Car G
£4688

Car H
£3577

> How much will the salesman make if he sells:

1 Cars A, D and E   2 Cars E, F and G   3 Cars A, B and E

4 Cars D, G and H   5 Cars F, B and H   6 Cars C, D and G

7 Which three cars should he sell to make the most money?
   How much is this?

8 Toby's car has done 8769 miles this year and 15778 miles
   last year. How many miles is this? It already had 69547
   miles on the clock – what does the clock show now?

> Copy and complete.

9
```
  4 7 6 8
  3 5 9 7
+ 4 8 7 8
```

10
```
  3 5 8 9
  2 8 7 5
+ 6 2 1 7
```

11
```
  6 5 2 5
  3 4 1 6
+ 8 5 3 4
```

12
```
  2 8 4 6
  6 2 8 5
+ 2 3 8 1
```

> Three amounts add to make £10 000. Two
> amounts are the same, and the other amount
> is greater than these. What are the amounts?

Adding

Choose your own method for these additions. Show your working.

I.
```
 4683+4000
 8683 -30
 =8653
```

1 4683 + 3970		2 15678 + 28572
3 22375 + 22868		4 19648 + 775
5 3766 + 3247		6 128365 + 368457
7 12564 + 32268		8 1235 + 6584
9 36571 + 12364		10 6785 + 3452

Fill in the missing numbers.

II.
```
    4 7 5 8
  + 7 5 8 6
  1 2 3 4 4
    1 1 1
```

11
```
   4 7 5 8
 +□5 8 6
 1 2 □□□
```

12
```
   6 3 7 2
 + 7 □9 6
 □□2 □□
     1 1
```

13
```
   8 7 6 5
 + 9 4 □□
 □□□4 0
    1 1 1
```

14
```
   7 8 5 3
 + 3 7 □6
 1 □□9 9
   1
```

15
```
   6 4 8 2
 +□□9 6
 1 2 2 □□
    1 1
```

16
```
   5 4 9 7
 + 8 6 □5
 □□1 2 □
    1 1 1
```

Each letter is a single digit. No digit is represented by more than 1 letter, e.g. if N = 2 no other letter can be 2. Give each letter a digit to make this addition work:

```
  R A I N
+ S N O W
S L E E T
```

Adding

> Copy and complete.

1.	5
	U t
	1·6
	+ 2·7
	4·3
	1

1	U t	2	U t	3	U t
	1·6		3·8		7·7
	+ 2·7		+ 5·7		+ 9·5

4	U t	5	U t	6	U t	7	U t
	8·5		7·6		6·8		5·4
	+ 5·7		+ 6·5		+ 4·4		+ 6·7

Dictionary
4·6 cm

Super Sums
5·8 cm

Fairy Tales
6·7 cm

Footy Facts
7·9 cm

Monster
Mayhem
3·8 cm

Dinosaur
Stories
5·5 cm

> How much shelf space is needed for these books?

8.		4·6
	+	5·8
		10·4 cm
		1

8   Dictionary and Super Sums

9   Footy Facts and Dinosaur Stories

10   Fairy Tales and Monster Mayhem   11   Footy Facts and Super Sums

12   Dictionary and Fairy Tales   13   Dinosaur Stories and Super Sums

14   Which pair of books takes up the most shelf space? The least?

> Find two fat books in the classroom. Measure their widths. How much shelf space do you need for them?

Adding

Each builder has two lengths of cable. How much in total?

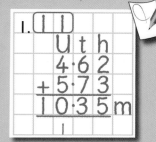

1.
U	t	h
4	·6	2
+5	·7	3
10	·3	5	m

1

4·62 m   5·73 m

2

4·87 m   6·11 m

3

6·27 m   3·92 m

4

5·92 m   3·64 m

5

4·38 m   7·43 m

6

5·64 m   3·84 m

7

6·29 m   1·47 m

8

4·72 m   3·56 m

Copy and complete.

9.
	8	
3	·8	2
+4	·4	8
8	·3	0

9   3·82 + 4·48 =

10   5·71 + 2·46 =

11   4·64 + 3·38 =

12   7·54 + 1·67 =

13   6·47 + 7·43 =

14   4·36 + 5·39 =

15   5·67 + 5·56 =

16   6·78 + 4·25 =

17   5·48 + 2·26 =

18   4·37 + 6·29 =

19   7·56 + 6·81 =

20   3·67 + 8·58 =

1·2 + 2·3 + 3·4 = 6·9. Can you find 2·3 + 3·4 + 4·5 = ☐?
How about 3·4 + 4·5 + 5·6? Keep going with
similar additions. What do you notice?

Adding

1 > Choose three CDs. Find the total cost. Repeat 10 times.

POP CLASSICS £4·59

£5·68

£9·87

£7·38

£7·64

£5·57

1.	£2	4	
	£	9·8	7
	£	5·6	8
+	£	7·3	8
	£2	2·9	3
		1	2

2 Which three CDs cost the most? How much do they cost?

3 Which three CDs cost the least? How much do they cost?

 > I bought three CDs using two notes. The change is 39p. Which CDs did I buy?

4 Craig is 48·5 inches tall. He stands 61·4 inches up a ladder. How high is his head?

5 Hilda bought a tent for £38·75 and a sleeping bag for £29·65. How much change did she have from £100?

6 Gita lives 4·8 km from Ghopal. Ghopal lives 5·6 km from Umesh, who lives 6·5 km from Basanti. How far must Gita go to visit them all?

> Copy and complete.

7 14·68 + 25·59 = ☐

8 23·95 + 36·87 = ☐

9 48·84 + 36·97 = ☐

10 55·97 + 43·85 = ☐

11 12·59 + 8 + 7·3 = ☐

12 14·53 + 9·17 = ☐

13 3·82 + 10.37 + 1·66 = ☐

14 4·25 + 12·68 + 3·27 = ☐

Adding

Fill in the missing numbers.

```
1.   3 6 4 7
   +   5 6 9
     4 2 1 6
       | | |
```

1
```
    3 6·4 7
  +   5·□ 9
    □ □·1 □
      | | |
```

2
```
  □ □ 7·8 5
  + 1 7·7 6
  1 3 □·□ □
      | | |
```

3
```
    1 6·5 8
  + 4 3·□ 7
    □ □·6 □
```

4
```
    2 7·6 3
  +   □·4 2
    3 2·0 □
      | |
```

5
```
    1 8·□ 2
  + 1 6·3 8
    □ □·3 □
      | | |
```

6
```
    4 2·8 9
  + 1 □·2 □
    □ 2·□ 3
      | | |
```

7
```
    4 7·□ 6
  + □ 1·2 9
    6 □·6 □
        |
```

8
```
    6 1·2 7
  + 1 2·□ 6
    □ □·1 □
      | |
```

9
```
    □ 7·8 5
  + 2 2·3 1
    6 □·□ □
      | |
```

10
```
    1 2·3 8
  +   9·□ 2
    □ □·8 □
      | | |
```

11
```
    1 □·2 7
  + 2 4·9 6
    □ 3·□ □
      | | |
```

12
```
    2 1·6 5
  + 1 8·□ 8
    □ □·4 □
      | | |
```

13
```
    3 2·7 9
  +   □·7 3
    3 7·5 □
      | |
```

14
```
    2 7·3 4
  + 1 6·□ 3
    □ □·1 □
      | |
```

15
```
    □ 4·3 8
  + 2 7·4 6
    8 □·□ □
      | |
```

16
```
    6 7·5 4
  +   8·□ 5
    □ □·4 □
      | |
```

Explore

Use one of each of digit cards 0–9 arranged like this:

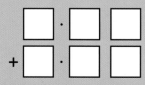

Try to make the total as near to 10 as possible.
Can you reach 10 exactly?

Subtracting

How much further to go?

1.
```
      2 0 0
       6  1
    3 7̶ 2̶
  − 1 6 8
    2 0 4  miles
```

1 Journey 372 miles
  Done 168 miles

2 Journey 683 miles
  Done 329 miles

3 Journey 492 miles
  Done 227 miles

4 Journey 871 miles
  Done 436 miles

5 Journey 683 miles
  Done 325 miles

6 Journey 792 miles
  Done 244 miles

7 Journey 983 miles
  Done 826 miles

8 Journey 674 miles
  Done 238 miles

9 Journey 462 miles
  Done 219 miles

How far has the hot air balloon fallen?

10 Was 816 m
   Now 542 m

11 Was 907 m
   Now 261 m

12 Was 828 m
   Now 453 m

13 Was 719 m
   Now 256 m

14 Was 836 m
   Now 382 m

15 Was 948 m
   Now 295 m

16 Was 827 m
   Now 586 m

17 Was 639 m
   Now 265 m

What is the largest 3-digit number that can be
added to two other 3-digit numbers to make 999?

27

Subtracting

Each holiday-maker drops off their hire car. How many miles did they drive?

1.
```
  4000
  7 1
  8 2 3 2
- 4 4 1 1
  3 8 2 1 km
```

1
Was 4411 km
Now 8232 km

2
Was 3273 km
Now 7528 km

3
Was 3246 km
Now 8672 km

4
Was 1263 km
Now 6838 km

5
Was 3429 km
Now 7863 km

6
Was 1827 km
Now 5639 km

7
Was 4395 km
Now 8678 km

8
Was 2842 km
Now 7363 km

Copy and complete.

9
```
  6 4 7 2
- 3 8 2 6
```

10
```
  4 8 3 4
- 2 1 4 6
```

11
```
  5 7 6 2
- 1 2 9 8
```

12
```
  8 3 6 3
- 2 6 4 9
```

13
```
  7 2 8 1
- 3 9 3 7
```

14
```
  7 4 8 2
- 4 7 4 6
```

15
```
  5 3 7 4
- 2 8 1 9
```

16
```
  9 6 7 3
- 4 8 5 7
```

□□□□ - □□□□ = 999.

Find numbers to make this subtraction work where neither number is a multiple of 10.

Subtracting

Each piece of jewellery is reduced. How much is it now?

1.
	3	5	
£	4	0	6	1
−£	2	8	3	2
£	1	2	2	9

1

Was £4061
£2832 off

2

Was £7403
£4189 off

3

Was £6074
£4638 off

4

Was £8053
£6645 off

5

Was £6502
£3679 off

6

Was £5082
£2674 off

7

Was £8604
£4793 off

8

Was £4206
£2589 off

9 Zack drove 4673 km on a trip across Europe. Becky took a shorter route, driving 3582 km. How much further did Zack drive?

10 The Chang family saved £1746 for the family holiday. It actually cost £2108. How much more did they have to pay?

11 Laura had collected 4318 ml of rainwater in her barrel. She use 2569 ml to water the roses. How much was left?

Check these additions using subtraction.

12.
	6	3	3	
	7	4	4	1
−	4	6	5	8
	2	7	8	3

12 4658 + 2783 = 7441   13 5387 + 2872 = 8259

14 6539 + 1873 = 8412   15 3634 + 2795 = 6429   16 1738 + 6873 = 8611

17 3694 + 3578 = 7272   18 5678 + 3946 = 9624   19 2795 + 5483 = 8278

 Two 3-digit numbers have a total of 851 and a difference of 113. What are the numbers?

Subtracting

Choose a method to complete these subtractions.

1.
```
    2 6 8 8
  +   3 1 2
    3 0 0 0
```

1.
```
    4 0 7 2
  - 2 6 8 8
```

1   4072 – 2688   2   3115 – 1551

3   5683 – 2864   4   6207 – 398

5   6861 – 2378   6   4083 – 3298

7   5396 – 527   8   7834 – 2356

9   6459 + 2374 – 3466

Explore

Write a 4-digit number.	4863
Reverse the digits.	3684
Subtract the smaller number from the larger number.	4863 – 3684 = 1179
Reverse the digits.	9711
Add the two numbers.	1179 + 9711 = 10 890

Repeat this 10 times. Explore the patterns.

True or false?

10   Subtracting 999 from 2033 leaves less than 1000.

11   The Battle of Hastings (1066) took place 900 years before England won the World Cup (1966).

12   5612 is 3462 more than 1150.

13   The difference between 4024 and 2044 is 1980.

Subtracting

How much more has:

I.		£4·60	

$$£2·80 + £0·20 = £3·00$$
$$£3·00 + £1·60 = £4·60$$
$$£1·80$$

1 Kelly than Sunil

2 Sunil than Becky

3 Lin Yao than Aleesha

4 Aleesha than Becky

5 Kelly than Aleesha

6 Lin Yao than Kelly?

Kelly
£4·60

Sunil
£2·80

Lin Yao
£5·10

Aleesha
£3·70

Becky
£1·90

How much more have:

7 Kelly and Sunil than Aleesha and Becky

8 Kelly and Lin Yao than Sunil and Aleesha?

How much in the purse now?

9  £6·08

Spends £3·98

10   £8·07

Spends £6·96

11  £7·04

Spends £5·87

12  £6·06

Spends £3·97

13 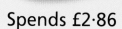 £5·03

Spends £2·86

14  £6·05

Spends £4·94

15  £4·02

Spends £1·88

16  £8·09

Spends £5·98

 Exactly how many times can £9·99 be subtracted from £100? What is left at the end?

Subtracting

Write how much each T-shirt is reduced by.

1.

			£ 3·2 3		
£ 1·8 6	+	£ 0·1 4	=	£ 2·0 0	
£ 2·0 0	+	£ 1·2 3	=	£ 3·2 3	
			£ 1·3 7		

1
£1·86
£3·23

2
£2·78
£4·35

3
£1·76
£2·34

4
£1·88
£3·21

5
£2·96
£4·22

6
£3·75
£5·43

7
£2·86
£4·25

8
£1·79
£3·32

9
£3·87
£5·34

 You save £1·25 on a T-shirt, which is a 25% saving. What could the original and the sale prices be?

Copy and complete.

10
£ 4·7 6
− £ 2·4 8

11
£ 8·2 7
− £ 4·7 3

12
£ 7·6 3
− £ 3·2 6

13
£ 6·5 4
− £ 3·4 8

14
£ 5·4 2
− £ 3·9 1

15
£ 3·5 6
− £ 2·7 4

16
£ 6·7 8
− £ 3·4 9

17
£ 8·2 6
− £ 5·4 1

Subtracting

How much has each plant grown?

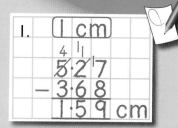

1. 1 cm

$$\begin{array}{r} 5.\overset{4}{2}\overset{1}{7} \\ -3.68 \\ \hline 1.59 \end{array}\text{ cm}$$

1

Was 3·68 cm
Now 5·27 cm

2

Was 4·79 cm
Now 6·38 cm

3
Was 3·87 cm
Now 5·43 cm

4

Was 2·79 cm
Now 6·42 cm

5

Was 4·86 cm
Now 5·23 cm

6

Was 4·67 cm
Now 7·54 cm

7

Was 5·58 cm
Now 8·32 cm

8

Was 4·36 cm
Now 6·24 cm

9

Was 5·74 cm
Now 7·43 cm

Choose your favourite method to complete these subtractions. Show your workings.

10 5·14 – 3·71

11 4·48 – 3·09

12 7·34 – 6·75

13 4·76 – 1·9

14 6·8 – 3·42

15 4·02 – 3·89

Subtracting

This is Lucy's homework. Check it for mistakes. Write out correctly any that she got wrong.

	¹ ¹1 ¹4			¹3			² ¹3 ¹1
1	2̷ 2̷ 8̷ ³3	2	1̷ ¹3 4̷ ¹2	3	3̷ 4̷ 2̷ ³3
	− 8 8 4		− 7 8 9		− 6 5 7
	1 3 7 9		6 5 3		2 7 6 6

	⁵ ¹2 ¹1			³ ¹1 ¹4			² ¹3
4	6̷ 3̷ 2̷ ⁴4	5	4̷ 2̷ 8̷ ³3	6	3̷ ⁶6 4̷ ²2
	− 7 9 5		− 6 8 4		− 7 7 8
	5 5 3 9		3 5 6 9		2 9 6 5

Find the missing numbers.

7	1 2·3 4	8	2 4·5 1	9	1 9·6 3	10	1 7·2 9
	− ●·7 ●		− 6·● ●		− 7·8 ●		− ●·6 ●
	4·● 6		● ●·1 5		● ●·● 8		1 1·● 5
	1						

11	2 1·6 4	12	1 5·8 3	13	2 3·7 5	14	1 8·3 4
	− 7·● ●		− 4·● ●		− 8·● ●		− ●·3 ●
	● ●·8 1		● ●·2 6		● ●·7 8		1 2·● 8

🔍 Explore

Write a 4-digit number with identical digits.	2222
Write a 3-digit number with identical digits.	666

The size of the digits in the second number must be larger than the digits in the first number.

| Take away the smaller from the larger number. | 2222 − 666 |

Repeat. Look for patterns.

Probability

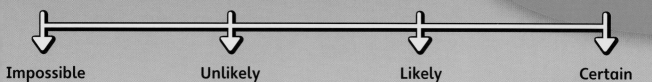

Impossible   Unlikely   Likely   Certain

Write one of the words above beside each statement.

1   I will land on Mars tonight.
2   I will go to bed late tonight.
3   I will walk more than 10 steps today.
4   My toenails will grow 10 cm this month.
5   I will be younger tomorrow than I am today.
6   My skin will become purple overnight.
7   I will find a four-leaf clover today.
8   I will watch television tonight.

Write two statements of your own for all four categories.

A coin is flipped 10 times. Write impossible, unlikely, likely or certain for each statement.

9   There were ten heads.
10   We had six tails and six heads.
11   More than four times the coin was tails.
12   Heads and tails came up equal.
13   One-quarter of the throws came up tails.
14   Six throws were tails.
15   There were fewer than three heads.
16   Eight were heads and four were tails.

Flip a coin ten times. Write down whether it is heads or tails each time. Do your results match any of the statements above?

Probability

The money box contains these seven coins. One coin falls out. Write impossible, unlikely, likely or certain for each.

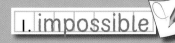

1. impossible

The coin falling out is:

1 a pound coin	2 a 50p coin
3 a 20p coin	4 a £2 coin
5 a 10p coin	6 worth more than 10p
7 a multiple of 10p	8 worth less than £1

Write certain, likely, unlikely or impossible for each statement.

In the UK:
9   It is hot in August.
10 It rains on more than two days in September.
11 It is cloudy in December.
12 It is sunny for all 28 days in February.
13 It rains for 31 days in June.

Put six coins in a purse. You must use three different types of coin. Try to make it likely that when you tip the purse a pound coin falls out.

No chance   Poor chance   Even chance   Good chance   Certain

Sarah takes one sock from her drawer. What chance is there that it is:

14 yellow	15 green	16 blue
17 not yellow	18 pink	19 either blue or green
20 not green	21 yellow, green or blue	22 yellow or blue?

Probability

No chance   Poor chance   Even chance   Good chance   Certain

Write one of these categories for each statement.

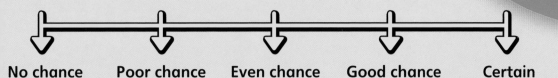
1. No chance

1   I will travel by rocket tomorrow.

2   I will travel on an aeroplane this year.

3   I will walk 20 miles this year.

4   I will use a computer today.

5   I will eat potatoes this month.

6   It will snow tomorrow.

7   I will go on a bus in June.

8   I will see a dragon tomorrow.

9   Write five statements of your own, one in each category.

Asif throws a 1–6 dice. What chance is there that the number it lands on is:

10   1

11   less than 4

12   7

13   odd

14   even

15   greater than 1

16   between 1 and 4

17   a whole number

18   $2\frac{1}{2}$?

 Work with a partner. Throw a dice 12 times. Look at your results. Would they be the same if you did it again? How might they differ?

Probability

Bag A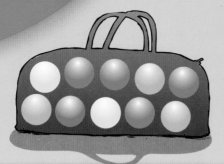

Bag B

One ball is taken from each bag. Which bag has the best chance of the ball being:

1   green   2   yellow   3   orange   4   blue

5   not green   6   not orange

7   either green or orange   8   either blue or yellow

9   pink   10 either yellow or green?

True or false?

11 When you throw a 1–6 dice, there is an even chance of getting a number less than 4.

12 It is impossible to get 6 sixes in a row when throwing a 1–6 dice.

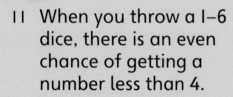

13 In Britain there is only a poor chance that there will be a month without a drop of rain.

14 There is a good chance that the 6:00pm news will contain a story about animals.

15 If you spin a coin twice, you have a good chance of getting heads twice.

16 If you drop a piece of toast there is a good chance that it will land butter side down.

 Look around your class. How likely is it that someone's first name will have more than two vowels?

Line graphs

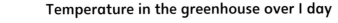

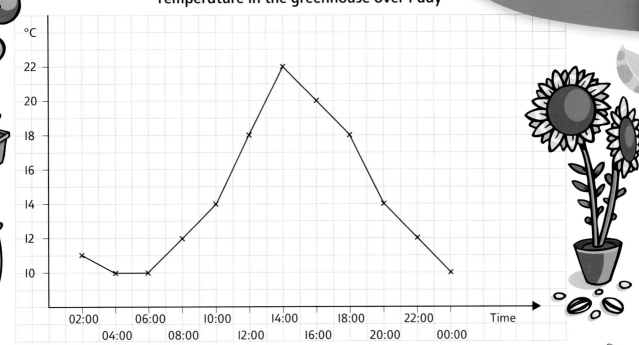

Temperature in the greenhouse over I day

At what times is the temperature: 1. 0 4 : 0 0 ...

I   10°   2   12°   3   18°   4   14°   5   22°   6   20°?

When is the temperature:

7   highest   8   lowest   9   half-way between 12° and 20°?

What is the temperature at:

10 04:00   II 02:00   12 20:00   13 00:00

14 08:00   15 16:00   16 22:00   17 12:00?

What is the approximate temperature at:

18 07:00   19 19:00   20 13:00   21 11:00?

Draw a graph giving the approximate temperatures
in your classroom over the school day.

Growth in a house plant each month

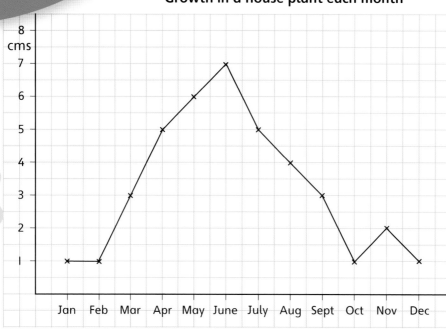

In which months did the plant grow:

1. June

| 1 | most | 2 | more than 4 cm | 3 | less than 3 cm |

4 least   5 between 4 cm and 8 cm   6 1 cm

7 less than the month before   8 unexpectedly more than the previous month?

How many centimetres did the plant grow:

9 between June and September   10 in August

11 in December   12 after July   13 before April

14 in May   15 in winter

16 in months without a letter 'r' in their name?

Sketch a graph showing the growth in your height over the last 5 years. What do you think it will be for the next 5 years?

Line graphs

Level of water in the Teign River in March

Date	1	3	5	7	9	11	13	15	17	19	21	23	25	27	29	31
Water level (cm)	85	85·5	86	88	87	89	93	94	94	93	90	89	87·5	89	90	89·5

1

Draw a line graph to represent this information.

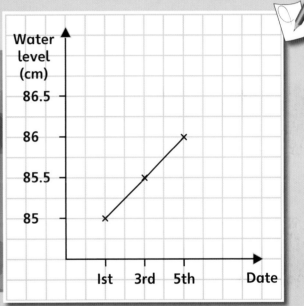

On what date was the water level:

2   highest   3   lowest

4   half-way between highest and lowest?

What was the water level on:

5   March 11th   6   March 23rd   7   the first and last day of March?

Write a brief news report about the weather in March in the Teign area.

Litres and millilitres

Write the number of millilitres in each container.

1. $\dfrac{1}{2} l = 500 ml$

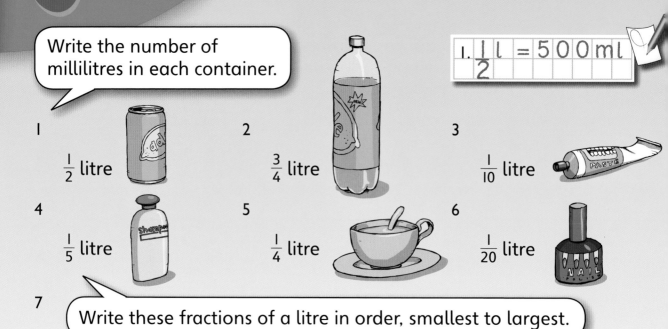

1 $\dfrac{1}{2}$ litre

2 $\dfrac{3}{4}$ litre

3 $\dfrac{1}{10}$ litre

4 $\dfrac{1}{5}$ litre

5 $\dfrac{1}{4}$ litre

6 $\dfrac{1}{20}$ litre

7 Write these fractions of a litre in order, smallest to largest.

Read each scale. Write each in millilitres. Write each as a fraction of a litre.

8. $500 ml = \dfrac{1}{2}$ litre

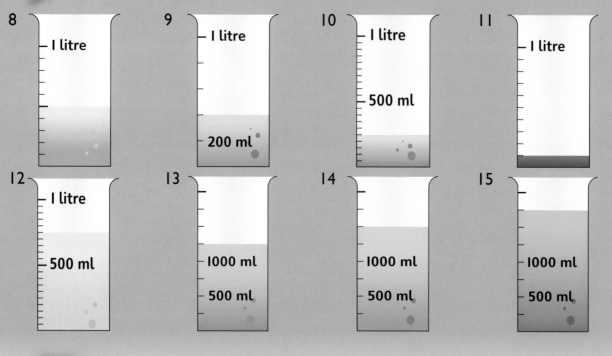

8 — 1 litre

9 — 1 litre
— 200 ml

10 — 1 litre
— 500 ml

11 — 1 litre

12 — 1 litre
— 500 ml

13 — 1000 ml
— 500 ml

14 — 1000 ml
— 500 ml

15 — 1000 ml
— 500 ml

A drinks can holds 330 ml. Estimate how much you drink in a day. How much in a week?

Litres and millilitres

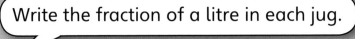

Write the fraction of a litre in each jug.

1. $100\,ml = \dfrac{1}{10}\,l$

1  100 ml

2  500 ml

3  250 ml

4 200 ml

5  750 ml

6 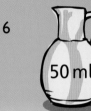 50 ml

Write each quantity of liquid as a mixed number.

7. $1 \cdot 5\,l = 1\dfrac{1}{2}\,litres$

7  1·5 l

8  1·75 l

9 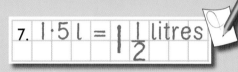 1·25 l

10  1·1 l

11  2·25 l

12  3·75 l

Combine the amount in each pair of containers. Write the total in millilitres.

13  $\frac{1}{4}\,l$ $\frac{1}{2}\,l$

16 $\frac{1}{4}\,l$ $\frac{2}{5}\,l$

14  $\frac{1}{10}\,l$ $\frac{3}{4}\,l$

17 $\frac{1}{4}\,l$ $\frac{1}{5}\,l$

15 $\frac{1}{5}\,l$ $\frac{1}{10}\,l$

18  $\frac{3}{10}\,l$ $\frac{1}{2}\,l$

 Two containers together hold $\frac{3}{4}\,l$. One holds 300 ml more than the other. How much do they each hold?

Litres, millilitres, gallons and pints

Approximate each capacity in pints.

1. 500ml = 1 pint

Hint: A pint is approximately half a litre.

| 1 | 500 ml | 2 | 1·1 l | 3 | 220 ml | 4 | 110 ml | 5 | $\frac{3}{4}$ l | 6 | 2·1 l |

How much does each tractor need in gallons?

7. 90 litres = 20 gallons

Hint: 9 litres is approximately 2 gallons.

7
90 l

8
45 l

9
27 l

10
18 l

| 11 | 360 l | 12 | 54 l | 13 | 630 l | 14 | 81 l |

15 Ruth drinks 5 pints of tea each day. Her friend says that this is more than 3 litres! Is this true?

16 Nevis the dog has a bath in the garden. It holds 12 gallons. She splashes half on the grass. How many litres are left in the bath?

17 A train uses 100 gallons of fuel on a journey. How many litres is this? If fuel costs 50p per litre, how much did the journey cost?

Make up your own word problem about litres and gallons.

Litres, millilitres, gallons and pints

Write the approximate equivalent in litres.

Hint: 2 gallons is 9 litres.

1. 1 0 gallons = 4 5 l

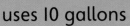

1 uses 10 gallons

2 uses 8 gallons

3 uses 20 gallons

4 uses 30 gallons

5 uses 16 gallons

6 uses 24 gallons

Which container holds more in each pair?

7   a $\frac{1}{2}$ pint   b 0·75 l

8   a 1 gallon   b 7000 ml

9   a 3 pints   b 1·5 l

10   a $\frac{3}{4}$ litre   b 1 pint

11   a $\frac{1}{4}$ pint   b 150 ml

12   a 4 gallons   b 15 l

13   a 4 litres   b 10 pints

14   a 2 gallons   b 20 l

15   a 8 pints   b 6 l

Approximately how many hair washes do you get from a 300 ml bottle of shampoo? How many bottles do you use in 1 year?

45

Angles

Write the size of these angles in degrees.

1
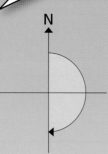

2

3
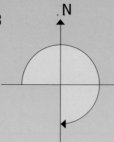

4
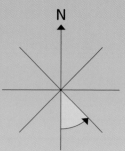

5
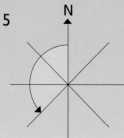

6
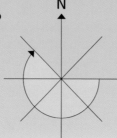

7
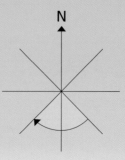

8
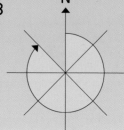

Write the size of these angles in degrees.

9

10

11

12

13

14

Find the angle that the minute hand will turn through when you are watching each of your favourite television programmes.

Angles

Write the angles measured by these protractors.

1
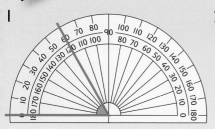

2
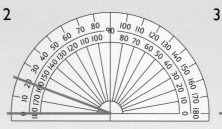

3
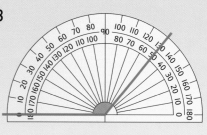

4
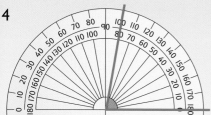

5
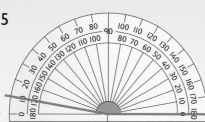

6
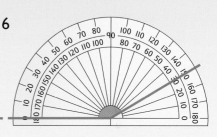

For each cake slice: (a) estimate the angle and (b) measure the angle. How good are your estimates?

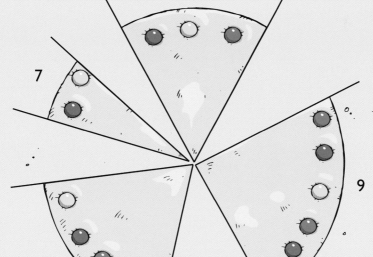

What is the angle of each slice if a cake has been cut into three equal slices? What about 4, 5, 6 … equal slices?

Angles

Write the approximate angle shown on each protractor.

1.⬚3⬚5°

1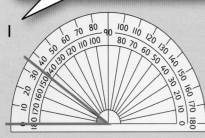

2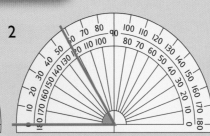

3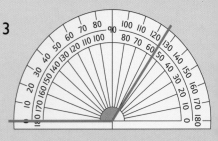

4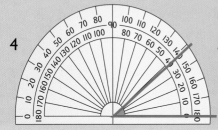

5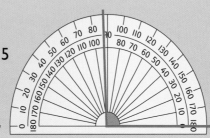

6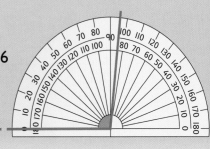

Draw these angles.

7   65°   8   125°   9   38°   10 101°

11 77°   12 141°   13 19°   14 89°

15

Draw round a large regular pentagon. Measure each angle and check that they are all equal.

Repeat for other regular polygons.

Draw an irregular pentagon where the angles are all different. Measure each angle. Can you draw another irregular pentagon, this time with a right angle?

Angles

1 Measure the angles of these triangles.

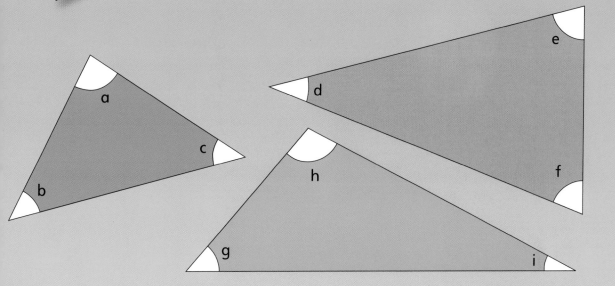

2 Find the total of the three angles of each triangle. What do you notice?

3 Draw three large triangles. Measure the size of each angle. What do you notice?

 **Explore**

Draw a large quadrilateral.

Measure the size of each angle.

Add them together.

Repeat for other quadrilaterals.

Write about anything you notice.

Angles

> Write the missing angle.

1
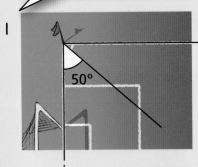
50°

2
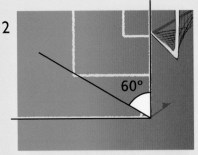
60°

3
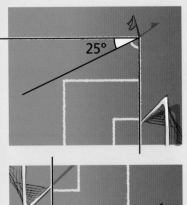
25°

4
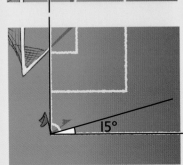
15°

5
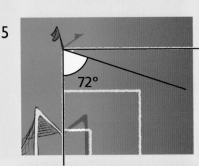
72°

6
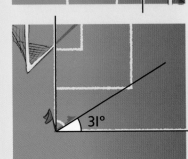
31°

> Two angles make a right angle. If this is the size of one, write the size of the other.

7   17°   8   63°   9   45°   10   57°

11   8°   12   34°   13   81°   14   73°

> Three angles make a right angle. If these are the sizes of the first two, write the size of the third angle.

15   24°, 17°   16   29°, 37°   17   42°, 17°

18   53°, 28°   19   8°, 69°   20   11°, 44°

> Draw a straight line from the corner of a sheet of paper to create two angles. Estimate their size, then measure. Check that they total 90°. Compare them with your partner's.

Angles

Write the missing angle.

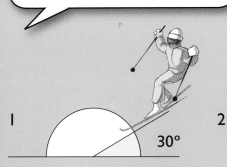

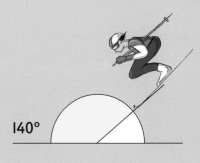

1 30°   2 45°   3 140°

4 170°   5 25°   6 165°

7 32°   8 157°   9 169°

Two angles make a straight line. If this is the size of one, write the size of the other.

10 46°   11 98°   12 113°   13 75°

14 57°   15 179°   16 144°   17 38°

Three angles make a straight line. If these are the sizes of the first two, write the size of the third angle.

18 56°, 73°   19 45°, 91°   20 114°, 38°

21 107°, 44°   22 84°, 19°   23 56°, 78°

 Look around your classroom. Can you find two pairs of angles making a straight line? Can you find a pair where the angles are not 90°?

Write the missing angle.

1
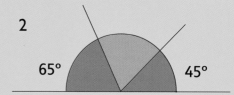
40°   30°

2
65°   45°

3
55°   96°

4
104°   48°

5
32°   126°

6
87°   64°

Two angles make a right angle. What are the angles if one is:

7 double the other   8 four times the other

9 five times the other   10 half of 40°

11 twice the size of 30° 12 four times 10°?

Explore

Three angles make a straight line.

What could they be if they are all multiples of 5°?

Angles

Write the size of each angle.

1. 1 0 5°, ...

1

0°
Empty

180°
Full

2

0°
Empty

180°
Full

3

0°
Empty

180°
Full

4

0°
Empty

180°
Full

5

0°
Empty

180°
Full

6

0°
Empty

180°
Full

 Explore

Use a large coordinate grid.

Draw a straight line from the origin (0, 0) to the point (5, 3).

Measure the angle made with the x-axis.

Calculate the angle made with the y-axis.

Repeat for lines drawn from the origin to other points, e.g. (1, 6), (6, 1), (3, 5).

Investigate any patterns.

Do some points make the same angles?

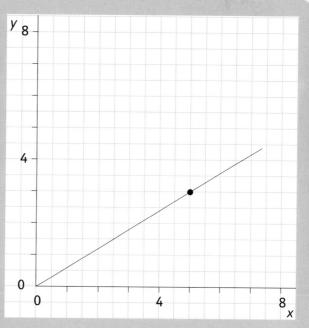

Acute, obtuse and reflex

1 Write 'acute', 'obtuse' or 'reflex' for each marked angle.

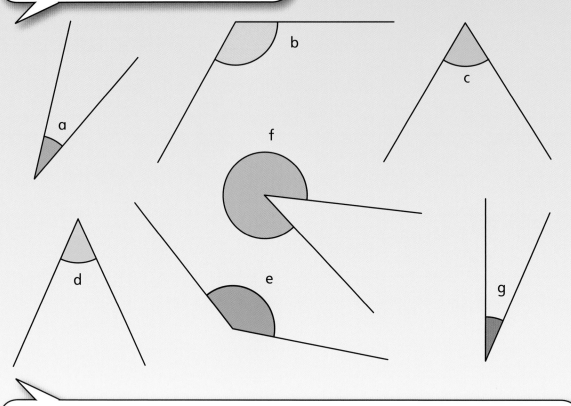

2 Estimate the size of each angle. Measure them using a protractor.

Draw an obtuse angle. Draw an acute angle that you estimate is half the size. Measure them both to see how good your estimate is.

Write 'acute', 'obtuse' or 'reflex' for each.

3	48°	4	140°	5	220°	6	17°
7	109°	8	185°	9	97°	10	86°
11	178°	12	310°	13	45°	14	194°

Acute, obtuse and reflex

Sarah turns clockwise. What type of angle does she move if she goes from:

1. acute

1	N to NE	2	E to SW	3	SE to S
4	NW to NE	5	SW to E	6	N to NW
7	NE to E	8	N to SE	9	SE to SW?

Write acute, obtuse, reflex or right angle each time.

10.(a) acute

10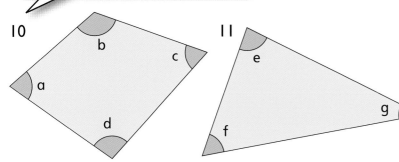

11

12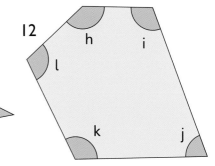

13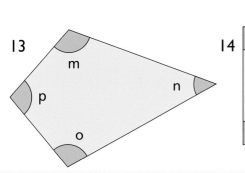

14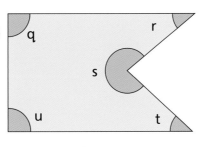

15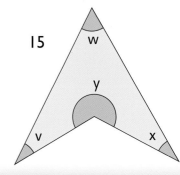

True or false?

16 The angles of an isosceles triangle are all acute angles.

17 The angles of a regular hexagon are all obtuse angles.

18 A triangle cannot have more than one obtuse angle.

Acute, obtuse and reflex

Look at the smaller angle between the hands of a clock at these times. Write the type of angle.

1. acute

 1

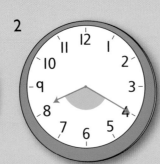 2

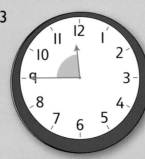 3

 4

5   quarter past 2

6   quarter to 10

7   8 o'clock

8   half past 11

9   half past 4

10   quarter to 8

11   06:20   12   01:35   13   04:00   14   02:45   15   10:55

16   Is it true that the larger angle between the hands on each clock is always reflex?

 Estimate as accurately as you can the times when the hands are in a straight line.

Draw these polygons.

17   a triangle with three acute angles

18   a triangle with two acute and one obtuse angle

19   a quadrilateral with two acute and two obtuse angles

20   a quadrilateral with three acute and one obtuse angle

21   a quadrilateral with one reflex angle

Acute, obtuse and reflex

Copy and complete the table to show the types of angle in each polygon.

	Acute	Right angle	Obtuse	Reflex
1	2	1	0	0

1 2 3 4 5 6

7 8 9 10 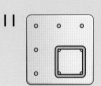 11 12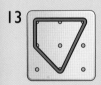

13 14 15  16  17 18

19 20 21 22 23 24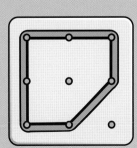

Explore

Investigate the angles in different pentagons drawn on a 3 × 3 grid.

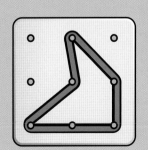

Write an estimate for the cost of each call.

$1. 80p \div 4 = 20p$

1   83p for
    4 calls

2   67p for
    3 calls

3   97p for
    5 calls

4   72p for
    6 calls

5   91p for
    4 calls

6   93p for
    7 calls

7   107p for
    5 calls

8   125p for
    6 calls

9   157p for
    8 calls

 Write some divisions that will
have an estimated answer of 20.

Copy and complete.

10
$63 \div 4$ (1 5)
```
    6 3
  − 4 0   10 × 4
  ───────
    2 3
  ───────  ... × 4
```
$63 \div 4 = \boxed{}$

11
$55 \div 3$ (⬭)
```
    5 5
  − 3 0   10 × 3
  ───────
  ───────  ... × 3
```
$55 \div 3 = \boxed{}$

12
$87 \div 5$ (⬭)
```
    8 7
  − ...   10 × 5
  ───────
  ───────  ... × 5
```
$87 \div 5 = \boxed{}$

13 $75 \div 4 = \boxed{}$

14 $55 \div 4 = \boxed{}$

15 $91 \div 6 = \boxed{}$

16 $67 \div 4 = \boxed{}$

17 $96 \div 8 = \boxed{}$

18 $59 \div 3 = \boxed{}$

19 $66 \div 5 = \boxed{}$

20 $87 \div 6 = \boxed{}$

Dividing

Write how long it takes to finish reading these books.

```
 1.   20

    1 2 7
   - 5 0    1 0 × 5
    ───
    7 7
   - 5 0    1 0 × 5
    ───
    2 7
   - 2 5      5 × 5
    ───
      2
    ─────────────────
    1 2 7 ÷ 5 = 2 5 r 2
    2 6 days
```

1 127 pages

5 pages a day

2 97 pages

4 pages a day

3 88 pages

3 pages a day

4 113 pages

6 pages a day

5 154 pages

9 pages a day

6 173 pages
   7 pages a day

7 129 pages
   5 pages a day

8 185 pages
   8 pages a day

9 203 pages
   6 pages a day

10 187 pages
    4 pages a day

11 206 pages
    8 pages a day

Find some long books. Work out how long it will take to read them at 4 pages per day.

Complete these divisions.

12 77 ÷ 3   13 113 ÷ 4   14 123 ÷ 5   15 147 ÷ 6   16 183 ÷ 7

17 107 ÷ 4   18 121 ÷ 5   19 203 ÷ 8   20 164 ÷ 3   21 139 ÷ 6

Write the length of side of each square field.

1. Perimeter = 96 m
2. P = 173 m
3. P = 251 m

```
1.  [2 5]
        9 6
     - ...   10 × 4
      . . .
      . . .
```

These gardens are regular polygons. Write the length of side of each.

4 P = 191 m

5 P = 151 m

6 P = 183 m
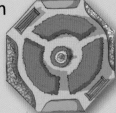

7 P = 173 m

8 P = 158 m

9 P = 134 m
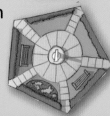

A lawn is the shape of a regular polygon. It has a perimeter of 217 m. What could the length of the side of the lawn be?

10 A taxi can take 4 passengers. How many taxis are needed for 71 children?

11 A number divided by 6 gives an answer of 5. What is the number?

12 Anna has 143 photos. An album holds 28 photos. How many albums does she need?

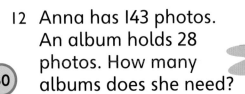

13 The CD rack can fit 7 CDs in each section. Shami has 165 CDs. How many sections will she fill?

Dividing

Complete these divisions.

1. 88 ÷ 3

2. 104 ÷ 6

3. 167 ÷ 7

4. 5)183

```
I.   30
     88
   - 30    10 × 3
     58
   - 30    10 × 3
     28
   - 27     9 × 3
      1
     88 ÷ 3 = 29 r 1
```

5. 8)241

6. 4)175

7. 119 ÷ 5

8. 7)213

9. 204 ÷ 9

10. $\frac{143}{8}$

11. $\frac{163}{9}$

12. 7 × ☐ = 372

 Explore

The answer to a division is 23 r 2.

If the number you divide by is a 1-digit number, what could the division be?

13. Estimate which of these is the largest, and which is the smallest. Find each answer, then put them in order, smallest first.

a. one-third of 82

b. one-quarter of 115

c. one-fifth of 263

d. $\frac{1}{8}$ of 147

e. $\frac{1}{6}$ × 107

f. $\frac{1}{9}$ of 300

g. $\frac{216}{4}$

h. $\frac{2}{3}$ of 246

Dividing

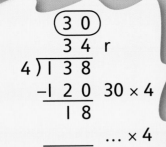
Copy and complete.

1
```
       (3 0)
         3 4   r
    4)1 3 8
    -1 2 0   30 × 4
      1 8
    ____  ... × 4
```

2
```
         (    )
             r
    5)1 9 6
    -1 5 0   30 × 5
    ____  ... × 5
```

3
```
         (    )
             r
    5)2 2 3
    -____   40 × 5
    ____  ... × 5
```

4 6)191

5 4)173

6 3)221

7 5)316

8 4)190

9 6)487

10 4)363

11 3)284

12 5)367

Write how many weeks it takes to save:

13 £165 at £3 a week

14 £233 at £4 a week

15 £191 at £7 a week

16 £346 at £5 a week

17 £213 at £6 a week

18 £471 at £8 a week

Investigate how many weeks it takes to save £500 at different rates.

Dividing

Crackers are packed in boxes. Find how many boxes.

1. [140]

```
      1 3 9 r 1
   4)5 5 7
    -4 0 0      1 0 0 × 4
     1 5 7
    -1 2 0       3 0 × 4
       3 7
    -  3 6        9 × 4
         1
```

1 557 crackers

boxes of 4

2 613 crackers

boxes of 5

3 728 crackers

boxes of 6

4 513 crackers

boxes of 3

5 873 crackers

boxes of 7

6 922 crackers
boxes of 6

7 742 crackers
boxes of 3

8 937 crackers
boxes of 7

9 925 crackers
boxes of 7

10 496 crackers
boxes of 3

11 870 crackers
boxes of 3

One-eighth of all crackers don't make a bang.
How many of the total number of crackers are faulty?

Complete these divisions. Estimate first.

12 4)913

13 7)854

14 3)726

15 5)681

16 2)739

17 6)904

18 3)858

19 4)703

20 2)937

12. [200]

```
      2 2 8 r 1
   4)9 1 3
    -8 0 0      2 0 0 × 4
     1 1 3
    -  8 0       2 0 × 4
       3 3
    -  3 2        8 × 4
         1
```

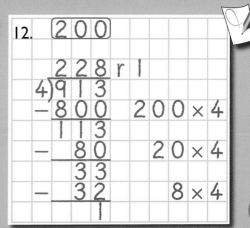

Dividing

1 Spring Water bottles are packed in sixes. 835 bottles are sent to the supermarket. How many packs of bottles is this?

2 Which is the greater prize: one-third of £826 or one-quarter of £947, and by how much?

3 Bina drinks lots of water. Last year she drank 937 pints of water. How many gallons is this? (Hint: there are 8 pints in 1 gallon.)

4 Kate's number, divided by 3, gives an answer of 279 r 1. Paul's number, divided by 4, gives an answer of 236 r 3. What are the numbers? Which is larger and by how much?

÷3

÷4

This is Lizzie's homework. Check each multiplication by dividing. Correct any mistakes, showing your working.

5 $4 \times 76 = 304$
$304 \div 4 = \ldots$

6 $3 \times 92 = 268$
$268 \div 3 = \ldots$

7 $5 \times 163 = 815$
$\ldots \div \ldots = \ldots$

8 $3 \times 217 = 681$
$\ldots \div \ldots = \ldots$

This is Sanjay's homework. Check each division by multiplying. Correct any mistakes, showing your working.

9 $258 \div 3 = 86$
$86 \times 3 = \ldots$

10 $670 \div 5 = 134$
$134 \times 5 = \ldots$

11 $888 \div 4 = 217$
$\ldots \times \ldots = \ldots$

12 $894 \div 6 = 133$
$\ldots \times \ldots = \ldots$

Dieviding

Check that 256 gives a remainder of 1 when divided by 3.

Investigate how many numbers between 200 and 300 also give a remainder of 1 when divided by 3.

How many give a remainder of 2?

Investigate how many give different remainders when divided by 4 or 5.

Complete these divisions, writing remainders as fractions.

1.
```
      1 5 0
      1 4 5   2
   3)4 3 7   3
   -3 0 0      1 0 0 × 3
     1 3 7
   -1 2 0       4 0 × 3
       1 7
   -   1 5        5 × 3
        2
```

1 3)437   2 4)914   3 2)739

4 5)652   5 6)743   6 4)861

7 7)916   8 3)838   9 4)1058

Find divisions that have these answers.

10 $47\frac{3}{4}$ 11 $38\frac{2}{3}$ 12 $56\frac{4}{5}$

13 $117\frac{5}{6}$ 14 $148\frac{1}{3}$ 15 $157\frac{1}{4}$

Fractions and decimals

Write as a decimal the coloured part of each square.

1 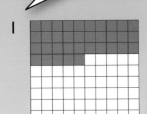   2 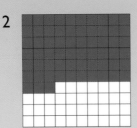   3 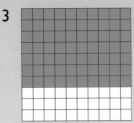   4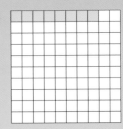

5 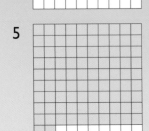   6 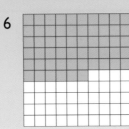   7 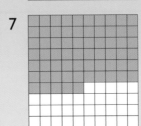   8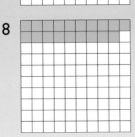

Write each part as a fraction.

1. $\dfrac{35}{100}$

Write each decimal as a fraction of a kilometre.

9. $0 \cdot 7 = \dfrac{7}{10}$ km

9   0·7 km   10   0·5 km   11   0·75 km   12   0·3 km

13   0·2 km   14   0·25 km   15   0·6 km   16   0·8 km

17   0·9 km   18   0·4 km   19   0·1 km   20   0·71 km

Explore

Choose from these seven coins to make different amounts.

How many different amounts can you make?

Write each as a decimal and as a fraction, e.g. £2·75 = £2$\frac{3}{4}$.

Fractions and decimals

Write as a decimal the length of each crocodile in metres.

1. $1\dfrac{35}{100} = 1\cdot35\,\text{m}$

1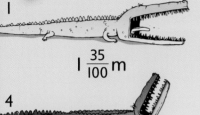

$1\dfrac{35}{100}\,\text{m}$

2

$2\dfrac{6}{10}\,\text{m}$

3

$3\dfrac{17}{100}\,\text{m}$

4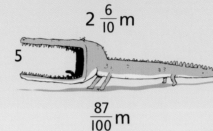

$1\dfrac{80}{100}\,\text{m}$

5

$\dfrac{87}{100}\,\text{m}$

6

$135\,\text{cm}$

7

$1\dfrac{1}{5}\,\text{m}$

8

$2\dfrac{3}{4}\,\text{m}$

9

$3\dfrac{1}{4}\,\text{m}$

 With a partner, measure your height in metres and write it as a decimal. Repeat for the distance between your fingertips when your arms are out sideways.

Find an equivalent number of tenths or hundredths for each fraction, then write it as a decimal.

10. $\dfrac{1}{2} = \dfrac{5}{10} = 0\cdot5$

10 $\dfrac{1}{2}$ **11** $\dfrac{3}{10}$ **12** $\dfrac{1}{4}$ **13** $\dfrac{3}{5}$ **14** $\dfrac{3}{4}$ **15** $\dfrac{7}{20}$

16 $\dfrac{11}{50}$ **17** $\dfrac{9}{10}$ **18** $\dfrac{4}{5}$ **19** $\dfrac{17}{20}$ **20** $\dfrac{4}{25}$ **21** $\dfrac{37}{50}$

22 Simon and Sarita shared a savings jar containing £6·40. Simon took 0·6 of the money and Sarita the rest. How much did they each take?

23 In a competition Zara got $\dfrac{1}{4}$ of the £100 prize, Dee got $\dfrac{2}{5}$ and Bram got 0·3. When they turned each fraction into decimals they could see how much they each had. Find out how much. How much was left?

Fractions and decimals

Write the position of each pointer as a fraction and as a decimal.

1. (a) $2\frac{14}{100}$ 2·14

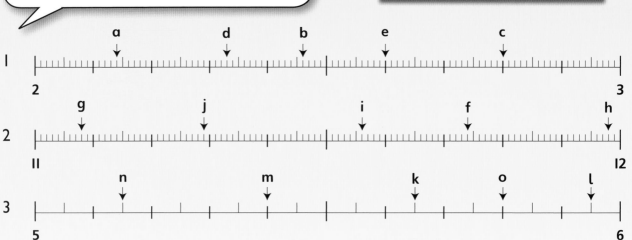

Write these in order, smallest to largest.

4 $3\frac{1}{4}$, $3\frac{7}{10}$, $3\frac{1}{2}$, $3\frac{26}{100}$, $3\frac{3}{4}$

5 $5\frac{18}{100}$, $5\frac{1}{10}$, $5\frac{1}{4}$, $5\frac{8}{10}$, $5\frac{8}{100}$

6 $1\frac{3}{5}$, $1\frac{3}{4}$, $1\frac{7}{10}$, $1\frac{65}{100}$, $1\frac{11}{20}$

7 $4\frac{21}{50}$, $4\frac{1}{2}$, $4\frac{9}{20}$, $4\frac{4}{10}$, $4\frac{3}{5}$

Use digit cards 0–9. What pairs of equivalent decimals and fractions can you make? For example:

$\boxed{0} \cdot \boxed{7} \boxed{5} = \dfrac{3}{4}$

Find each of these decimals as fractions. How many marbles?

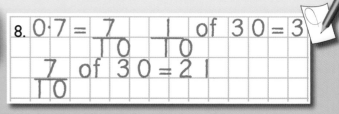

8. $0·7 = \dfrac{7}{10}$ $\dfrac{1}{10}$ of $30 = 3$

$\dfrac{7}{10}$ of $30 = 21$

30 marbles   8   0·7   9   0·8   10 0·3

36 marbles   11 0·25   12 0·75   13 0·5

50 marbles   14 0·1   15 0·9   16 0·6

Fractions and decimals

> Write <, > or = between each pair.

1. $2\frac{3}{5} = 2\frac{6}{10} = 2 \cdot 60$
   $2 \cdot 60 > 2 \cdot 57$

1   $2\frac{3}{5}$ $2 \cdot 57$ 2 $4\frac{1}{10}$ ⭐ $4 \cdot 09$

3   $3\frac{1}{4}$ ⭐ $3 \cdot 7$ 4 $5\frac{3}{4}$ ⭐ $5 \cdot 72$

5   $7\frac{63}{100}$ ⭐ $7\frac{6}{10}$ 6 $1\frac{45}{100}$ ⭐ $1 \cdot 4$

7   $6\frac{7}{10}$ ⭐ $6 \cdot 70$ 8 $8 \cdot 3$ ⭐ $8 \cdot 03$ 9 $4\frac{9}{100}$ ⭐ $4 \cdot 9$

Explore

Write some decimal numbers between 1 and 1·50, e.g. 1·01.

Write each as a mixed number, making the fraction as simple as possible.

$$1 \cdot 01 = 1\frac{1}{100}$$

$$1 \cdot 02 = 1\frac{2}{100} = 1\frac{1}{50}$$

Investigate how many of the hundredths you have written can be made simpler.

> Write the number half-way between:

10   1·2 and 1·32   11 $1\frac{3}{5}$ and 1·64

12   $4\frac{18}{100}$ and 4·2   13   3·65 and $3\frac{71}{100}$

14   4·9 and $5\frac{14}{100}$ 15   1·96 and $2\frac{1}{10}$

> How many pairs of decimal numbers are there between 0 and 1 that have reversed digits? For example, 0·43 and 0·34.

Percentages

Write the coloured percentage of each square.

1. 6 0 %

1 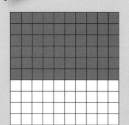 2 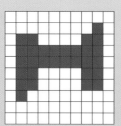 3 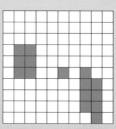 4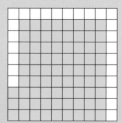

5 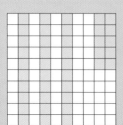 6 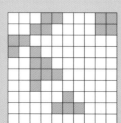 7 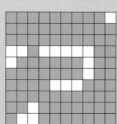 8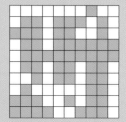

Write the percentage of each square that is not coloured.

1. 4 0 %

Draw a 10 × 10 square. Using whole squares, colour squares to make your initial. You must colour at least 20% of the grid.

Write these fractions as percentages.

9. 8 0 %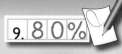

9 $\frac{80}{100}$ 10 $\frac{10}{100}$ 11 $\frac{45}{100}$ 12 $\frac{95}{100}$ 13 $\frac{1}{100}$

14 $\frac{1}{2}$ 15 $\frac{1}{4}$ 16 $\frac{3}{4}$ 17 $\frac{1}{5}$ 18 $\frac{7}{10}$

Write these percentages as two different fractions.

19. $\frac{30}{100} = \frac{3}{10}$

19 30%   20 25%   21 90%   22 20%

(70) 23 10%   24 75%   25 70%   26 110%

Percentages

Write the coloured percentage as a fraction and as a percentage.

1. $\frac{1}{2}$, 50%

1   2   3   4

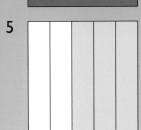 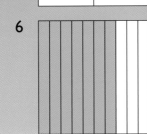 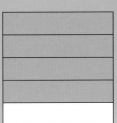 

5   6   7   8

How much is each prize worth?

9. 1st prize £25,
   2nd prize £12·50...

	Total	1st prize	2nd prize	3rd prize
9	£50	50%	25%	10%
10	£120	40%	30%	20%
11	£200	60%	25%	15%
12	£70	50%	20%	15%
13	£1000	55%	25%	15%

In each raffle, what percentage is left over? How much is this?

9. 15%, £7·50

Invent a raffle prize and split it between five winners, each with a different percentage. Find how much each winner received. Can you find a different way to split the prize?

Percentages

Write the new prices in the sale.

1. £20

1
Was £40
50% off

2
Was £50
20% off

3
Was £60
10% off

4
Was £80
25% off

5
Was £100
5% off

6
Was £20
40% off

7
Was £50
60% off

8
Was £40
15% off

For the first game, what other percentage price reductions would give a whole number of pounds off?

9 Rama spends 30% of his day sleeping, 25% at school, 10% watching television and 10% eating. How many hours does he have left for other activities?

10 In a book sale, all books have 50% off. Natalie bought four books with original prices of £4·50, £1·60, £12·80 and £3·40. How much did she save?

Write these in order, smallest to largest.

11 30% $\frac{1}{2}$ $\frac{3}{4}$ 60% $\frac{1}{4}$

12 $\frac{3}{5}$ 65% $\frac{3}{4}$ $\frac{7}{10}$ 55%

13 $\frac{1}{4}$ 35%   20% $\frac{3}{10}$ $\frac{8}{20}$

14 $\frac{3}{20}$ 21% $\frac{6}{25}$ 17% $\frac{9}{50}$

Percentages

1 Copy and complete the table.

	50%	10%	5%	1%
£80				
£120				
£60				
£90				

Use the table to help you find:

2 56% of £60

3 35% of £90

4 61% of £120

5 23% of £80

6 73% of £80

7 27% of £60

8 66% of £120

9 49% of £80

10 19% of £90

I am a number. Who am I?

11 I am 50% of a quarter of 32.

12 I am two-thirds of 60% of £50.

13 I am the difference between a third and 25% of £60.

14 I am exactly half-way between 25% of 80 cm and 40% of 120 cm.

You pay £20 for a jumper in the sale. It had been reduced by 50%. What was the original price? Now imagine it had been reduced by 20%. What was the original price? Explore other percentage price reductions.

Square numbers

Write the number of coupons in each set.

1. 25

1

2

3

4

5

6

7

Work with a partner. Estimate how many coupons between 100 and 200 can be arranged in a square. Now work it out!

Are these square numbers – yes or no?

8. No

8 12	9 16	10 20	11 32	12 81
13 48	14 1	15 86	16 36	17 50
18 71	19 100	20 60	21 64	22 90

Square numbers

Draw a picture to show how these pegs can be arranged in a square shape.

1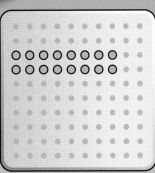

2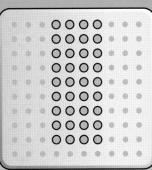

3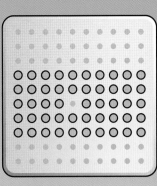

4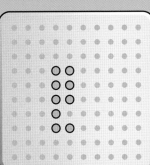

5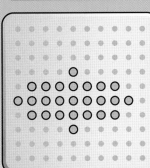

6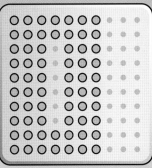

Copy and complete.

7   $4^2 =$

8   $7^2 =$

9   $2^2 =$

10   $9^2 =$

11   $6^2 =$

12   $8^2 =$

13   $5^2 =$

14   $1^2 =$

15   $3^2 =$

16   $10^2 =$

17   $0^2 =$

18   $11^2 =$

Explore

Use a set of 1–9 digit cards.

Make different square numbers.

How many can you make?
How many of the cards can you use?

| 3 | 6 | | 4 | 9 | | 1 |

five cards used

Square numbers

Write the next square number after:

1.116

| 1 | 11 | 2 | 46 | 3 | 39 | 4 | 17 | 5 | 50 |
| 6 | 20 | 7 | 82 | 8 | 75 | 9 | 62 | 10 | 28 |

Write the square number that comes before:

| 11 | 14 | 12 | 38 | 13 | 60 | 14 | 45 | 15 | 20 |
| 16 | 90 | 17 | 84 | 18 | 27 | 19 | 73 | 20 | 55 |

What is:

21 the seventh square number?

22 six less than eight squared?

23 one-quarter of six squared?

24 one-third of the square of nine?

25 the total of the third and fourth square numbers?

26 the difference between the fifth and ninth square numbers?

Explore

Write two consecutive square numbers.   25, 36

Find their difference.   36 − 25 = 11

Investigate patterns in the difference between consecutive square numbers.

Square numbers

> I am a square number. Who am I?

1 When I am multiplied by myself, the result is 81.

2 Both of my digits are multiples of 3.

3 My digits total 13.

4 I am 11 more than the previous square number.

5 I am the square of a quarter of a half of the eighth square number.

6 I am a 2-digit square number. Both my digits are even.

7 I am two square numbers that have a total of 100.

8 > Copy and complete this table of squares.

10^2	20^2	30^2	40^2	50^2	60^2	70^2	80^2	90^2	100^2
100									

 Explore

Write the square numbers in order. 1, 4, 9, 16, 25, …

Write the sequence of their units digits. 1, 4, 9, 6, 5, …

Continue the sequence. Look for patterns in the units digits.

Factors

For each block of stickers, write a pair of factors.

1. $12 = 2 \times 6$

1

2

3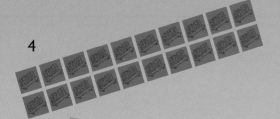

4

5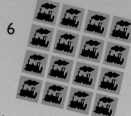

6

7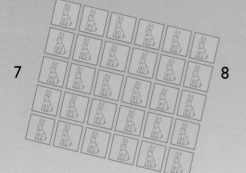

8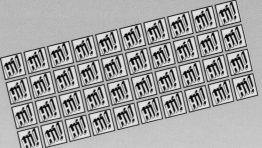

Draw another rectangle to match the number of stickers in each.

1.

Write the missing factor.

9   $16 = 8 \times \boxed{}$

10 $24 = 3 \times \boxed{}$

11 $20 = \boxed{} \times 5$

12 $18 = \boxed{} \times 3$

13 $35 = 5 \times \boxed{}$

14 $100 = \boxed{} \times 10$

15 $40 = 8 \times \boxed{}$

16 $42 = 7 \times \boxed{}$

17 $45 = 5 \times \boxed{}$

18 $63 = \boxed{} \times 7$

19 $24 = 2 \times \boxed{}$

20 $90 = \boxed{} \times 3$

Factors

For each number, complete the pairs of factors.

1 20 → 1 × ☐, 2 × ☐, 4 × ☐

2 18 → 1 × ☐, 2 × ☐, 3 × ☐

3 30 → 1 × ☐, 2 × ☐, 3 × ☐, 5 × ☐

4 14 → 1 × ☐, 2 × ☐

5 40 → 1 × ☐, 2 × ☐, 4 × ☐, 5 × ☐

6 32 → 1 × ☐, 2 × ☐, 4 × ☐

7 63 → 1 × ☐, 3 × ☐, 7 × ☐

8 34 → 1 × ☐, 2 × ☐

Use your answers to write a list of factors of each number.

The numbers 30 and 40 each have four pairs of factors. Investigate other numbers with four pairs of factors.

Write a list of all the factors of these numbers.

9 **6**   10 **16**   11 **10**   12 **50**   13 **28**   14 **48**   15 **60**   16 **52**

Find a missing factor in each set.

17 Factors of 12
   1   2
  6   12   4

18 Factors of 20
  1   5   20
    2   10

19 Factors of 18
   1   18
  6 2   3

20 Factors of 28
   1   14
   4   2

21 Factors of 15
   3   5
     15

22 Factors of 40
   4 1 2
  8 20 10 40

Factors

Change one number into a pair of factors before multiplying.

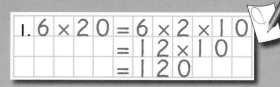

1. $6 \times 20 = 6 \times 2 \times 10$
$ = 12 \times 10$
$ = 120$

1   $6 \times 20 = 6 \times 2 \times$ 🌼

2   $4 \times 30 = 4 \times 3 \times$ 🌼

3   $6 \times 15 = 6 \times$ 🌼 $\times$ 🌼

4   $5 \times 12 = 5 \times$ 🌼 $\times$ 🌼

5   $12 \times 35 =$ 🌼

6   $14 \times 25 =$ 🌼

7   $9 \times 18 =$ 🌼

8   $18 \times 12 =$ 🌼

9   $25 \times 24 =$ 🌼

10   $15 \times 36 =$ 🌼

Who am I?

11   I am a factor of 18. I am a square number.

12   I am a factor of 32. I am half a square number.

13   I have only two factors. I am between 20 and 28.

14   I have an odd number of factors. I am between 30 and 40.

15   I am a factor of 50. I am an odd number. I am not a multiple of 5.

16   I have exactly three factors. I am between 5 and 20.

Explore

16 is a square number.

Its factors are: 1, 2, 4, 8, 16

So it has five factors.

Investigate the factors of square numbers.

What patterns do you notice?